# BAD MACHINERY

## THE CASE OF THE GOOD BOY

ONI PRESS

AN ONI PRESS PUBLICATION

# BAD MACHINERY™

## THE CASE OF THE GOOD BOY

### By
### John Allison

Edited by
James Lucas Jones & Jill Beaton

Designed by
Keith Wood & Jason Storey

Oni Press, Inc.

*publisher,* Joe Nozemack

*editor in chief,* James Lucas Jones

*art director,* Keith Wood

*director of publicity,* John Schork

*director of sales,* Cheyenne Allott

*editor,* Jill Beaton

*editor,* Charlie Chu

*digital prepress lead,* Troy Look

*graphic designer,* Jason Storey

*administrative assistant,* Robin Herrera

Oni Press, Inc.
1305 SE Martin Luther King Jr. Blvd.
Suite A
Portland, OR 97214

onipress.com
badmachinery.com

Become our fan on Facebook: facebook.com/onipress
Follow us on Twitter: @onipress
onipress.tumblr.com

ISBN: 978-1-62010-114-8   /   eISBN: 978-1-62010-115-5

Library of Congress Control Number: 2012953355

First Edition: February 2014

20 19 18 17 16 15 14 13 12 11 10 9 8 7 6 5 4 3 2 1

Printed in China.

CHARLOTTE

JACK

SHAUNA

LINTON

MILDRED

SONNY

CHARLOTTE GROTE! You're making the place look untidy.

What NO mum, I am being educational.

GRAB

Take the dog out for a walk. He's forgotten what the sun looks like.

Pepper, see, that orange circle is the sun.

It's a big ball of gas what will one day turn red and destroy us all.

Probably out of anger that sunbeds have stolen all its tanning business.

# FIGHT!

ARCH-DUKE
GRR-DINAND

LADY
PROBLEMS

Okay so we're going to the carnival on Friday night.

Oh no you're not

Yes.

Friday's when the older kids go, Jack. Teenagers. You won't be safe.

Why, Jessica?

You'll get your heads bashed in. Like soft boiled eggs.

Go on Saturday afternoon.

You think we'll embarrass you.

NO

Well yeah. And you wouldn't like it.

They turn the baby rides off after 6 o'clock.

We have to go then. Sonny has Naturecraft Folk on Saturday.

Well it's your funeral. Funerals.

Wait, what's "Naturecraft Folk"?

Sonny do not tell her what Naturecraft Folk is.

It's–

Mum, he's too little to under-stand fairgrounds.

He'll get confused and wet himself.

BORB GROUND WEE!

We took you to the carnival and you loved it.

MUMMMM NO!

Even after you wet yourself.

FINE.

FINE.

Yeahhhh!

Who's this HUNK?

BOTTY

Mildred, I have to warn you, if he hasn't got nits at the moment...

...he's think-ing about getting them later.

RUFFLE

RAF RAF RAF RAF

Ah-hah-hah hah

I see Mildred and Pepper are now in love.

It is natural. Pepper is the best dog.

He is a mongrel, that is the best breed.

Lottie a mongrel isn't a breed. That's when it's not any sort of dog.

He's obviously sort of a dog. He's not a *parrot*.

Let's find Pepper a wife so he can have puppies!

Puppies for me!

Sorry Mildred but Pepper has been "sorted out".

His test icicles are in heaven.

Did you... have a funeral for them?

No but Mum said we wouldn't eat meatballs for a month.

Out of RESPECK.

Shauna it is CRUEL not to take Humphrey on the teacups.

Charlotte later we will get out the postage stamp...

...on what you have written everything you know about babies.

HARSH.

Look at him. He seems quiet, he is smiling a bit.

Do you know what will change all that?

Spinning him round uncontrollably for two minutes.

But it's slow... fun! Baby fun!

No. He only has a basic sort of mind. Like a pigeon's mind.

To him the teacup ride would be like a comb'nation nucular attack an' bad hair day.

He wouldn't know what end to start leakin' out of first.

You like Pepper, don't you Mildred?

I like everything about him. *Everything.*

I MUST HAVE IT

What are you lookin' at?

THAT

OH that! That is there every year. I don't think it's real.

Win it if you can! Try where a million others have FAILED!

Win...

How is it enchanted? Tell me that first.

Whatever it draws, whatever it writes, comes true!

Has Pepper given Mildred rabies? She looks mad.

She's gonna try for the magic pencil! You know she's a good shot!

Oh yes, the magic pencil game. That is good value.

I believe it is impossible to buy a bigger load of old toss for £2.

Yeh I'm thinking about giving up the magic pencil.

No money in it any more.

My grandpa had this attraction, and my dad.

People just don't believe in the power of an enchanted pencil any more.

BUGSY MALONE

But I've got PLANS.

Hillbilly Simulater

I know, stick to the pencil.

Sigh.

Roll up! Roll up!

I WANT TO PLAY

KARAOKE
MINI FRIDG

PLOP

VEP

ROLL

POF

What.

I think it might be fixed, Mildred.

WORK TO RUL

I WANT TO PLAY AGAIN.

Listen um, Jack sorry, we...

DON'T WANT TO TALK ABOUT IT.

I want to go on THAT.

The Obliterator 500?

I really don't want to-

Yeah we'll go on it with you, sure.

It spins you round in three different directions at once.

Linton I don't feel good about this ride.

Look Sonny, when you get off you're treated like you just got back from *war*.

This is all you think about now.

Stop bickering. When we've been on this ride no one can say we're soft.

It says it exerts 5 gees, what's a "gee"?

It stands for "GAS".

WAIT HERE

I woke up this morning and felt my lip split.

Knew it was going to be a bad day.

BRAP BRAP

That's pretty good isn't it, Humphrey?

TO THINK Shauna said this ride was humiliatin' to even *stand near*.

It seems decent to me.

SIFFER

Yeah she's all right, your sister. What's she up to?

Oh! Helping sort out a local dispute!

THIS IS A FIX! A FIX!

Come on Mildred, you're just mad because you've blown 12 quid...

No! This is fixed!

There is something wrong with your BALLS!

Cor, you're worse than Charlotte.

Clear off you two, sling your hooks.

Listen! It's a booth where you can win a crayon that "grants wishes".

BUT

There's not an exact legal point where he has to be straight with you.

Boys, disgusting *boys*.

I worked it out, Shauna, there is a reason Jack Finch is so quiet.

CHIPS
FISH
PIE
CHEESE
PUDDING

SCRAPS

If he walks and talks at once, he just falls over.

Well um I think that Jack—

OH HUMPHREY AARGH

I *tole* you, boys are *disgusting*.

And now it's raining.

He's wet inside and he's wet outside.

Come on, my brother stinks, Mildred's skint and it's chucking it down.

I'm going to stay and have one more go at the magic pencil. Bye Pepper.

You should hold his bum up towards the rain to rinse him off.

Or dunk it in a puddle.

I'm going to ask a roadsweeper to drive over him. Very gently.

Now it's really good of you guys to chase off the smokers AND stomp out their cigs.

We were worried about their health.

Yeh, sir.

They like you. They think you're cool.

Well they ain't meant to!

I don't dress like this for my health!

A good teacher I figure should be sort of unpleasant but *reliable*.

SMOULDER

SMOULDER

Is that...?

Corrrr

I told you I'd get it! I told you!

Mildred, what have I told you about standing on the table?

That's right, nothing.

Errr

Because it seems like something that would never need saying under any circumstances.

OPERA NORTH

SCOTT WALK

"TILT" ON ICE

*Mildred* I am basically going to DIE if we don't try out the magic pencil soon.

OK but it seems to me there are rules for this sort of thing.

Have you ever read "The Monkey's Paw"?

Like palm reading? Seems too easy. "In the future you will eat a banana."

No, it's a story where a man gets a paw that grants wishes.

Except everything he wishes for brings bad luck!

I've read it! It ends with him as a mad zombie knockin' on the door!

YES. So we have to be careful.

I've decided to draw a dog, as helping animals is not selfish.

No, that seems all right.

Mildred you should rub that out.

If scientists ever find that thing they'll have to get rid of evolution and start from scratch.

"TILT" ON ICE

What are we meant to do?

Search for every cigarette? Wet 'em with a jug?

The rules of smoke patrol ain't that well defined!

Calm down. It'll be fine.

BACK INSIDE EVERYBODY

Okay so we're wishin' for a speedboat and a network of underground tunnels...

...and harem pants.

Lottie!

Aren't you afraid of the monkey's paw?

That paw is not gonna get me.

If it comes after me I'll hit it with a tennis racquet.

Do one of you two have the pencil?

No!

HEADMASTER

That got ugly FAST.

# Four more little tykes disappear

**by Erin Winters**

The "Little Tykes" nursery in Keane End has been closed after four more children vanished - taking the total to nine.

Nursery manager Susan Bovis was at a loss to explain the disappearances of Toby Milton, Verity Bates, Sam Shaw and Abbie Cottram (all aged 2).

"One minute they were there, and the next they weren't," she said. "Little ones are always wandering off. I'm sure they'll come back. They're probably having a wonderful time."

Despite Ms Bovis' lack of concern, parents seem reluctant to return their children to her care.

Police are treating the disappearances as suspicious, but sought to reassure locals that the vanished children are the exception, rather than the rule.

DCI Mike Carver of Tackleford Police was confident that the children would be found.

"There are thousands of children in Tackleford Metro-polital Borough, but only nine have vanished in the last three weeks."

"I've got a couple of officers keeping an eye out. They'll turn up."

### BEAST

Some locals have linked the disappearances to recent sightings of a "hairy beast" around dusk.

Pub landlady Elaine Hirst claims to have seen the creature crouching in a back alley.

"When it saw me, it ran away. It might have been a big dog, or a panther, but scruffy," she said.

"I only got a quick look but it scared the life out of me."

DCI Carver was quick to quash these "beast rumours".

"Sightings of beasts and big cats usually turn out to be overweight domestic pets," he warned.

"We urge people not to become hysterical if they can possibly avoid it."

Do you want to play some games?

I'm not allowed computer games ...on account of them promoting *violent* stereotypes.

SO IT IS IMPORTANT THAT WE PLAY THEM ALL *NOW*.

Let's see, I've got—

WE'RE PLAYING UNICORN FRENZY AND WE'RE PLAYING IT *NOW*.

0

5000

60

10059075

SOD FRENZY

Jack how did you get that black eye?

Playing rugby.

I don't believe you.

Do you think I haven't seen you playing rugby?

Making sure the unoccupied part of the pitch isn't *lonely*.

I... walked into a door.

Eye first?

If you're going to lie, stick to the first lie.

Is someone bullying you Jack?

Because that is not okay with me at all.

Jack maybe I have pushed you round a bit over the years.

But no one messes with *my* personal punchbag.

Who is it Jack, who's bullying you?

It's nobody. It's nothing.

Is it Benny Marks?

Yes, it looks like nothing.

I don't know.

Does he look like a kind of human sausage?

He does, doesn't he?

I knew it.

I will sort this out.

No, you'll make it worse. He might just stop.

Why's he picking on you?

I *dunno.*

Well it doesn't matter. I'm going to talk to some people.

You didn't cry, did you?

You're going to be okay, Jack.

No, I let it out as swears like you taught me.

Shauna! Lottie's here to see you.

Tell her I don't want to see her!

Just go up, love. She's probably in one of her moods.

Shauna I didn't mean to scratch your face.

Mildred was pulling my tie so hard that I had gone into the SPASMS OF DEATH.

DEATH SPASMS!

Okay then, I forgive you.

Fancy fightin' over a flippin' "magic pencil".

Ugh. I know. Let's add it to the list of things we're not allowed to row about.

OK. Licking other people's yoghurt lids. Best singers.

Rules of tennis, "badmington", marbles, hula hoop.

Imaginary... magic... trinkets.

Hula hoop defo doesn't have rules, Lottie.

FORFEIT DANCE, NOW.

CLONK

BONK BONK

What is THAT?

ROW ROW ROW ROW

AAAAAAH!!!

Glenys Neil there was a was a—

AAAAAAH!!!

Would you like another oat cake, Archibald?

ROWR. RAF!

What are we going to do with that... thing?

Keep him! Keep him *forever*.

If I understand that look, and I think I do, we aren't keeping him forever.

We'll work it out this evening.

It's Parents' Evening this evening!

Here's the letter, sorry that it's quite old.

I'm not leaving it here on its own all day.

I'll work from home.

Okay. See you later.

Bye Archibald!

Are you even a dog?

HEY!

CLANG

I just caught someone trying to rob my van... AGAIN!

It says "no tools are left in the van overnight."

Stealers aren't good readers, Dan.

He left his crowbar though.

Whoa! Watch out crows!

Did he manage to get anything?

Your Velvet Underground tape?

No.

Well. Maybe he'll try again tomorrow.

Are you coming to Parents' Evening tonight?

No. I'm looking after Humphrey.

Yes! Keep him safe from the BABY SNATCHER, Shauna!

It's more about keeping him from banging his head into sharp corners.

*His favourite thing to do.*

Maybe he'll be a stunt man one day.

If he makes it to "man" we'll see about stunts.

Aw Jack, cheer up, parents' evening won't be bad for you. I heard of the six words you said all term, five of them were *great*.

LOTTIE. BE NICER.

I'm sure the teachers love your talking.

It's a non-stop reminder that they haven't gone deaf yet.

All right Jack.

Linton.

How's it going, Mr Finch?

Heh heh not bad!

PUMP

I wonder how my dad's going to embarrass me tonight.

Your dad's funny!

At least Mum's not here. It halves the danger.

Your mum and dad aren't HALF as bad as mine.

Has your mum ever tried to give you a big wet kiss in front of the girls' hockey team?

There's something wrong with her BRAIN.

You know what you are Dan? Soft.

No one's going to try to rob my van with 'im around.

Look at those teeth!

I'd rather not.

Are you sure it's not one of them banned dogs?

It's too fluffy. It's one of those mountain dogs, a Komondor.

Where's its tail?

Shauna, because you did so well this term, we got you a present.

What is it?

A dog!

Are you sure?

It looks *mental.*

Go on Shauna, say what you think.

I think it is going to poo like a LION.

I like it maybe 63%

Oh god, the *face* on her.

Get used to it. It's going to be there for a while.

We could have kept that dog, you know.

No we couldn't. I didn't tell you.

I took a phone call this morning and left Archibald in the kitchen.

I was gone twenty minutes or so.

When I came back, he was drinking... from a cup.

DOOK

DOOK

He'd knocked it onto the floor?

No, he was holding it like a person. It was *eerie.*

That's the DOG-GONEST thing I ever heard!

AWFUL.

A dad-joke that bad could get you kicked out of the *league of dads.*

It's out there... the *beast.*

Plucking babies from their cribs with its big, hairy fingers.

Taking a fresh batch back to its cave...

...or den, if all the local caves are occupied...

...FOR SOME CHEWING.

Do the prints lead anywhere?

Towards the woods. But there's not much of a trail.

See Linton, Naturecraft Folk taught me how to *track.*

I guess you have to take a break from singing and clapping sometime.

So who fancies a walk in the woods?

Nice beast avoidance, boys.

I saw Linton running and thought he'd seen something!

I... I thought I heard a faint cry for help coming from the park.

It turned out to be just the wind, but...

Hm yes better safe than sorry.

Listen.

The babies of today are idiots, but tomorrow they could be scientists.

We will save them.

My plan involves identifying the beast, trapping it, and... and...

...STUFFING IT AS A WARNING TO OTHER CREATURES.

Whoa! Intense!

Maybe *too* intense!

Do you have any better suggestions?

*Egg it in the town square.*

Oooaaah keep that thing away from me! The racist dog!

I thought that was Mildred's dog.

Hm well my stepdad got it off her dad, to guard his van.

He's called Archie.

ROW!

How can you tell it's a boy?

The obvious way.

He prefers BLUE.

We're... we're investigating the Tackleford Beast!

Jack! That's dangerous!

Don't care.

It's a mystery for *men*.

Well be careful.

HUH, there's your beast right there.

I'll smack you, Linton!

Jack, he means the dog!

Wooooo!

Okay, to lure this beast, we need a baby or a... toddler.

Right right, we'll just go down the supermarket and get one... *wait.*

Sonny!

WHAT? No!

Sonny, we'd just be *borrowing* your sister.

We wouldn't let the beast get her.

No! No no no no no no! NO!

We just want to get the beast out into the open, then we'd...

We'd chuck her over a fence so she'd be safe.

CHUCK HER OVER A FENCE?

He just has to get used to the idea.

It'll be a lot harder to "chuck her over a fence" when she's 47, Linton.

STOMP  STOMP  STOMP  STOMP  STOMP

Bad Machinery, Volume Two

Linton please don't tell that I almost drowned you.

It wasn't your fault that the bridge was rotted.

And if I hadn't been picking on you...

...you wouldn't have had to fight me.

Friends again?

Yeah, friends, ok.

It doesn't matter if Shauna likes you. I wish someone liked me.

She's a nice person.

Yeah she's nice, pretty nice.

I dunno.

What are you going to tell your mum and dad happened?

That I fell in the river for science, on the brink of a great discovery.

Ha ha yeah. "Baxters don't float."

You make a better door than a window, Jack.

At least I know how to get dressed.

YUR YUR YUR

Make yourself useful.

KNOCK KNOCK

KICK

Sonny!

Hello, Jack.

Linton?

Get in.

Put this on.

But my mum, I can't—

Your mum has been *informed*.

You're NATURE-CRAFT FOLK now.

Sonny what no, you are not getting us into your leaf-touching club.

23rd Annual NATURECRAFT FOLK CORROBOREE

This is Linton and Jack.

Welcome welcome!

Come in come in, we're always pleased to see newcomers.

Everybody, say hello to Linton and Jack, your newest *Salamanders*.

Salamanders! No!

Linton come on. At least you never had to be a *tad-pole* like Cecile.

All right every-one, time to sing the Naturecraft song.

WE GATHER IN THIS PLACE TODAY

TO THANK THE FRIENDLY EARTH

Someone told me that an animal will chew its own leg off to get out of a trap.

How could I not have understood.

...BREMBLY EARTH

Your friends seem to be enjoying themselves.

Yes. It just takes them a little while.

*To enjoy anything.*

What's *that*?

Well it started as an elephant.. then it sort of had a "mouse stage"...

...now I think it's one of those "shrunken heads".

Yeah, nice. I've made a GUN.

All right everybody, time to go inside and-

TIME TO...

OH NO

BEEP BEEP!

BEEP BEEP!

If Jack and I get married, I'll be MRS WICKLE FINCH.

Oh no... Wickle Finch, that's like, a baby bird.

*That won't do.*

AUUGGHH! WHO WAS THAT?

It's no one's fault, Jack. Everything Nature-craft Folk fed us was made of leaves or beans.

Anyway, come on, it's time.

Hey, don't be rough with her! She's delicate!

I'm being careful!

I know it took a lot for you to set this up.

Sorry Sonny.

Yes well, with you two fighting, someone had to get the beast caught.

Thanks. We know you could get into trouble.

Well there are going to be risks on a man's adventure!

And naps, apparently.

He's had a big day.

Some might say, Lottie, that the amount of THINGS attached to your phone...

...maybe make it less useful than it might be if it didn't weigh a ton.

Those people saying that would be INSANE.

My phone is the BEST.

I have an attack whistle, and a bottle opener, and a picture of us being friends...

Do you not like being *friends*?

Is it necessary to have a slightly smaller phone attached to it?

Listen Shauna, it is a statt-uss thing, you would not understand.

It just doesn't seem important.

Shauna, I have a HIGHLY DEVELOPED SENSE of what is important and...

YOU TWO HAVE TO COME WITH ME, NOW

Shush Mildred.

-and look, see, you are always going to need a *fan*.

It's my fault that beast is out there! Look! LOOK!

That's Archibald that Lottie drew...

...and that's THE BEAST

Wor yeah look at it and all.

What about Mildred's crummy dog face?

Crummy!!?

I don't think there are enough wishes in the world to make that thing real, haha.

Ha ha ha!

This is serious. I have unleashed a bloodthirsty creature.

Mine was nice. I made a nice one.

DRIIIIIINGG

And then I let someone steal the pencil, AGGHHHH

We have to find it and quick. Before someone uses it in...

In a... in a...

VAMPIRE DRAWING COMPETITION.

OK, so the magic pencil disappeared during the fire alarm.

If it wasn't nicked by a squirrel, it must have been someone from our class.

But *who*?

There's no point *arksing*, people're just gonna say they didn't whatever.

Maybe we can go through official channels.

Look at Mr Beckwith. He looks like him and Mrs Beckwith had all the wine last night.

He's goin' to make us sit down over pencil issues.

"Sit down Lottie other pencils are available and etc."

The culprit will give himself away.

Yeah like how you gave yourself away by drawing the most vi-lent beast of all time.

But who could it be?

WHO?

I told you, death from above was the only way.

It wasn't really death, Mildred, it was jumpin' on him and steal- ing back the pencil.

It's only death *eventually.*

You start with mild discomfort, then *build up.*

Well you got it back, now vow not to use it.

Give it to Shauna, she's the most boring one. She won't use it.

Oh boring, thanks.

Yeah, *boring.*

She means *sensible.*

Who's George got talkin' to them this morning?

A prominent local naturalist, talking about the Tackleford Beast!

That's suspi- ciously interesting, Miss Perks.

Do you think this is one of his... *friends?*

I didn't think he had "friends".

I thought maybe he drew smiley faces on the damp patches on the wall and named 'em.

Who's got two thumbs, speaks French, and has bagged every top predator on the planet?

That's right. MOI.

My name is Jesper Bloem and I am an international big game hunter.

What people don't realise is that hunters are also *conservationists*.

Yes we are.

BELUGA WHALE

AFRICAN ELEPHANT

MARINE TURTLE

If an animal goes extinct, you can't shoot at it, and that is a tragedy, children.

The continued existence of exotic species underpins the knife industry, the crossbow industry...

The stuffing industry!

Taxidemy is a noble art, little girl.

Did you ever try shooting a stuffed one?

Give me your phone, Lottie! I want to ask the hunter what Archie is.

Hello little girl, do you know what this is? A tiger's tooth.

Um yeah great... do you know what this animal is?

It's our "dog" but it's clever, and...

*Bombus Bombus*, the common dog, nothing more.

Oh well. Thanks.

He said Archie was nothin' special.

Oh.

Help me talk Mildred down from her rages before maths.

I FOUND THAT MAN OFFENSIVE IN EVERY WAY POSSIBLE.

Come on Mildew, unclench at least a couple of things or you'll stick that way.

I heard about Archie, Shauna, I'm really sorry-

Come on Jack. Women, eh? Women.

*Women.*

Once we trap the beast, she'll be impressed.

She'll forgive you for standing her up at the cinema.

Cecile's donated Brian Bunny to "help Linton".

Brian's so covered in kiddy spit and germs that the cheroonear won't be able to resist.

Wow, he's *gross.*

Now, I reckon we need to dig a deep pit to catch it.

Or we could drop a big steel cage on it.

*Yes.* We can use all that heavy digging and lifting machinery we *didn't get for Christmas.*

Or... we could stiffen it up with a load of hair-spray.

I found these little children lost and trembling in the woods.

Another moment and they'd have been dinner for the cheroonear.

WE WEREN'T LOST

WE WEREN'T TREMBLING

WE ALMOST CAUGHT IT

Push off, kids, the grown ups are talking.

Why don't you come for a drink with me, pretty lady, I'll tell you how I trapped 'im.

Blerg okay.

WE FLIPPING CAUGHT IT, ERIN WINTERS

AAARGH

Look at it, it looks so pathetic now.

Yeah, now it's not chewing baby bones.

We should get a souvenir.

Hmm. So we can remember the time we screamed like girls, FOREVER.

TAP TAP TAP

He's a brute, this one, isn't he? He almost had my hand off!

Hoo hoo! Boy oh boy!

ARROO!! ROW ROWWW ROWW!

WHAM

We'll let him stew for a bit.

Look at 'im. It's almost like 'e understands 'is predicament.

I conf'dently predict we will find your dog by tea time.

Don't make promises you can't keep, Lottie.

It's not like finding a slipper.

Put your faith in Pepper's beak! He's an excellent sniffer! EXCELLENT.

He barely even has a "beak".

HMPH. Well, either he finds Archibald, or takes us to a sausage factory.

One way or the other, it's somethin' to DO.

Look for Archie! He'll be stampeding too, he likes joining in!

Too many BEASTS!

Maybe we should wait for everything poisonous to leave first.

They aren't gonna bite us, Lottie.

They're either leggin' it...

...or looking for revenge on the zoo keeper.

PHOOT

PHOOT

Worr he's revenging back!

And no one's going to eat us?

FLUMP

Being in a zoo means getting fed.

That's the compensation for getting gawked at while you're doing your business.

STITCH

STITCH

SNUFF

SNUFF

Is this like when a wasp lands on you?

And you have to stay still until it goes?

SNUFF SNUFF SNUFF SNUFF SNUFF SNUFF

Um um um depends, can you think of ANY REASON...

...that a thing that likes the taste of *babies* would be interested in you?

SNUFF SNUFF SNIF SNUFF

*Oh Humphrey*

GLORRR

*HUMPHREY!*

HUMPHREY YOU ARE GOING TO THE ORPHANAGE

BORB!

AAAAAA!

AAAAAA!

What is THAT?

I... I donno!

It would be easier to tell if I could fit it all in my eyes at once!

WEIRD

WOM WOM WOM WOM

Flipping heck Shauna, go on!

PUSH

Jack?

AKMAL'S

Ohh Jack.

Jack why didn't you say something to me about getting bullied?

I don't know.

I've got a big dog.

And a big stepdad.

And a little brother with headlice.

We could have worked something out.

So Benny is gonna get expelled?

Yeah. Apparently he burned down the cricket pavilion.

I heard Mr Beckwith got it all out of him. All of it.

Wow, ole Beckwith is all right, isn't he?

Yes.

Okay, so we're agreed?

SHARPEN IT.

Goodbye, magic pencil.

BIMPO
ELECTROMATIC

It was too tempting to use it. No one should have that power.

SO, what shall we do now?

I guess we'll have to deal with the appearance of...

...THE WORLD'S LARGEST BOWL OF STRAWBERRIES AND CREAM!

MACK

Waiting... waiting...

Still waiting...

...all dat cream

On the A65 at Wasson, a lorryfull of strawberries has shed its load...

...causing a dairy truck to overturn. Expect tailbacks-

WHOA!

That pencil! *How did it work?*

SHAKE

SHAKE

MACK

Well I reckon, and this is a *guess*...

...that it kind of hexes you up to draw what's gonna happen anyway.

Or maybe it's a... focus for fate.

A FOCUS FOR FATE!

Waffly... vague... but *convincing*.

That's the tree where they buried Clarice Nutter.

The witch! All seeing!

See 'ow twisted it is!

TACKLEFORD, 1811

Aye, t'were ever thus, from a sapling.

They say you can see't future if you chew its bark.

But 'im as knows the future...

...is cursed to to live through it, knowin'.

Oh but the riches tha'd have, knowin' what happens tomorrow!

Come away Stanley, it's not worth it to try.

Hmm. Strong... splinter-resistant...

I'd be a d--n fool not to make a pencil out of this tree!

The Case of The Good Boy

128

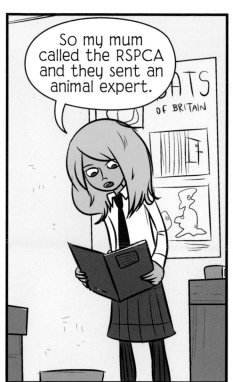

So my mum called the RSPCA and they sent an animal expert.

He said my dog Archie was actually a "wendigo"...

That is a sort of mad Canadian wolf-boy.

AGED 5

AGED 18

2.4 metres

They grow eight feet tall with teeth like pins so we could not keep him.

He had been imported illegally. Wendigos are very rare!

I was very sad when we said goodbye to him but he is better off in his natural habitat...

...the Canadian tundra.

There he can hunt yaks and live with his own kind. That's it.

Thanks Shauna. Very good.

I still reckon she could have raised him herself.

Yak isn't cheap Mildred. They're hard to catch and exc'llent hiders.

Your beloved wife is home from work, dear!

Another big day, bread on the table tonight!

Oh Ryan. You haven't even taken off your teacher clothes!

Aw, hell of a day, Amy.

Hell of a day.

We had to expel a lad today.

What did he do?

He'd been pushin' a lad around, a real nice little guy. Busted up his eye.

And he burned down the cricket pavilion.

So, hurray?

Nah, it all came out, you know? And this is his third secondary school, and-

Stop drinkin' my misery beer!

Misery tastes quite good!

So does Carol Perks still fancy you, Ryan?

Aw no, it ain't like that, wife.

It's just the friendship of colleagues. Colleague-ly.

Anyway, Perks has got a boyfriend.

An IMAGINARY boyfriend.

No he uh... manages a call centre.

CLICK

IMAGINARY call centre. IMAGINARY CALLS!

Invite them round for dinner.

"Oh KEN couldn't make it. He had to mend the call centre."

This is unchari-table. I am not impressed.

"7.00? Can we make it eight?"

"Only I need to pash my pillow embroidered with your husband's face for an hour."

What a rich fantasy life you lead.

Dear Jack
would you like to see
Hero Man 2 on Saturday?
If so meet ME outside

☆ SHAUNA ☆

**Charlotte Grote**

*"Well the good news is, I've gone
mad with fear now too."*

**Sonny Craven**

*"Well, there are going to be risks
on a man's adventure."*

**Jack Finch**

*"The babies of today are idiots, but
tomorrow they could be scientists."*

**Shauna Wickle**

*"Being in a zoo means getting fed. That's the compensation
for getting gawked at while you're doing your business."*

**Linton Baxter**

*"I wonder how my dad's going to
embarrass me tonight."*

**Mildred Haversham**

*"WE'RE PLAYING UNICORN FRENZY
AND WE'RE PLAYING IT NOW."*

GRISWALDS

EX VENTO SCIENTIA

EST. 1701

# GLOSSARY

Great Britain is an island and we have our own ways. Yes we are a simple people, but we are sophisticated enough to have made up our own versions of words and phrases just for us. I will take you through them and if you complain after this, it is your problem as far as I am concerned. We're not IDIOTS, they're just IDIOMS.

LOVE,
Charlotte
XXX

**Making the place look untidy:** This is when you have arranged yourself very neatly on the floor and then your mum trips over you and stubs her toe because she was not paying attention jeez louise.

**Nits:** Headlice. Now I have never had nits but if you do get them they put this shampoo on your head that smells like the curtains at an old folks' home. Bad news. Or they use the electric comb on you which, to be honest, sounds quite good. See also: "nit nurse." The Nit nurse is a woman who comes to school and checks your head for nits, she probably hates her life a great deal.

**Sick:** Vomit. It is a versatile word: "I felt sick, I sicked up on Grandma and now there is sick all over my Christmas presents."

**Mongrel:** what the Americans call a "mutt". That is, a dog what does not cost two grand while having weak lungs and then gets stolen by dog criminals. A mongrel is a better sort of dog.

**Skint:** Not having any UK pounds sterling.

**Test icicles:** Moth balls.

**Pram face:** a very unkind term used to describe a young mother who has not had the best of education and life opportunities etc.

**Cricket pavilion:** The house that cricketers go to to put their special outfits on. It is a rarefied zone with a special cupboard for the "boxes" they use to protect their test icicles. It is not beyond imagination to think that maybe while in the pavilion they go for a tinkle before the game. But as I have never been in a cricket pavilion, I do not know.

**Little tyke:** A young scamp. An annoying child who is probably also quite dirty and won't leave you alone.

**Chip off the old block:** an apple that has not fallen far from the tree.

**The Velvet Underground:** Music band from the past who caused all sorts of trouble. The sound of the Velvet Underground is like a set of bagpipes going through a mangle while a German exchange student lists all the reasons you should take up living homeless as a hobby. Bad news for people who like sounds.

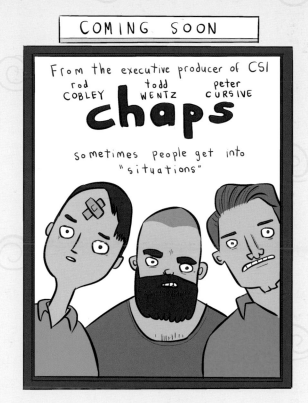

COMING SOON

From the executive producer of CSI

rod COBLEY  todd WENTZ  peter CURSIVE

**chaps**

sometimes people get into "situations"

**Cinema:** The movie theatre, where one goes to be richly entertained while enjoying food and drinks at prices that even a king would think was well out of order. Is popcorn actually food? No one has ever proved it.

**Pash:** Ferocious kissing. Spit everywhere.

**"You make a better door than a window":** Imagine that you are watching an improving and educational television programme such as *Keeping Up With Kim Kardashian's Lifestyle Choices* and then a family member stands in front of the screen and stops to have a think. This is what you say to them when this happens. It is a simple statement of fact and no one is offended.

**Fancy:** When you fancy someone, you want to pash 'em up. Fancying develops into various forms of relationship, such as love relationship, or hiding from someone relationship. You can also fancy a cup of tea but I think that is international.

**Lorryfull:** Metric version of a "trucksworth".

**Chippy:** Belligerent. "Don't get chippy with me, sunshine," is the sort of thing an imaginary Cockney taxi driver might say if you tell him he has gone the long way round and should have driven through the industrial estate thereby saving you £5.50.

**A load of old toss:** The kind of items one might discard without second thought.

**Quid:** One pound sterling. Basic human money for the United Kingdom.

**Badger:** Like a low-slung bear, but smaller.

# JESPER BLOEM
## (Master Hunter and Raconteur)

– recalls –

# THE ONES THAT GOT AWAY

**Beasts, critters, animals and natural miscellanea who avoided capture against all odds.**

I was born a baby in South Africa in the difficult years between the Great Struggle and the Big Push. Though my hands were small and weak, my father quickly pushed a crossbow into them and told me what to do. Before my first birthday, our humble mantlepiece featured a delicately stuffed bee. Sadly, that infant trophy burned, as so many things did, in the Huge Situation, but its memory will live as long as its life was short. Every Ahab has his whale, and here are mine. Eleven creatures who bested Bloem, and may yet best him again. Animals of wit, primitive intelligence, or luck. The ones that got away.

## Coulomb's Boar
### (Bombus Bombus)
### ENGLAND

Having made my home in England, I expected that there would be little to hunt besides rabbit, grouse and maybe a pheasant for the pot. But during a heathland ramble on my estate I came across the unfamiliar form of Coulomb's Boar. Packing only a shotgun, I was overcome by the thought of bacon, when a second boar butted me from behind, knocking me onto the ground where I stunned myself on a protruding stone. When I awoke, my shirt had been completely eaten away by the litle wretches. Bare-chested, I returned to the house for a larger and more vindictive weapon, but my manservant had prepared a delicious broth for lunch, so I nursed my sore head and cold breast by the fireside instead.

## Silver Tom
### (Bombus Bombus)
### SOUTH AFRICA

Some say that the Silver Tom is the cleverest ape, others that he is simply a man covered head to toe in fur, with a violently pink bottom. All I know is that for two years, Silver Tom was employed as my driver and valet. I have no idea how he hoodwinked me, but his erratic driving and abysmal ironing were offset by his wicked sense of fun. I have no wish to shoot Silver Tom, I simply wish to see his his furry face again, and share a banana with him as I did on many a pleasant evening years ago.

## Kraken
### (Bombus Bombus)
### ATLANTIC OCEAN

It is a brave man, or a fool, who does not respect the ocean. While hunting sharks off the coast of Cuba, the men aboard the ship began a great hullabaloo. I expected a beast of some variety, but could not have aniticipated a Kraken making its appearance. A hundred feet in girth, if not more, it lashed the boat with its tentacles, easily snapping it in two. As I drifted in open waters, waiting for rescue or the infinite, I was sustained by the thought of catching that sea monster, stuffing it, mounting it on a handsome plinth, and charging people to see it. I imagined a gift shop containing stuffed Kraken, sold at a handsome profit. Fortunately I was borne to safety by a man passing by in a coracle.

## Giraffe Snake
### (Bombus Bombus)
### JAPAN

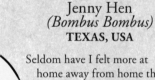

I have a powerful love for the Japanese people, with their culture founded on respect, politeness, efficiency, organisation, technology, and vicious feudal weaponry.

During a spiritual retreat in Nagoya, I took time out from my meditation to walk in a glorious flower garden. Resting beneath the wisteria, I felt a sudden slithering around my ankles, and saw a Giraffe Snake curling around my feet. Knowing it to be both venomous and quick to strike, I gently reached inside my kimono for a ceremonial dagger. Heart quickening at its silvery hiss, I positioned myself for the kill. It was to my great disappointment when the snake was suddenly vacuumed up by an elderly gentleman on a futuristic hovercraft.

## Jenny Hen
### (Bombus Bombus)
### TEXAS, USA

Seldom have I felt more at home away from home than among the big hats and big guns of Texas. Strolling amid the oil derricks, I caught sight of the Jenny Hen, a grossly elongated, flightless bird bred for its meat in the 1950s but ultimately deemed too weird and dangerous to be cooked for dinner. I took a couple of pot shots at it but managed only to explode a pile of oil barrels, to my hosts' evident delight.

### Tookey's Possum
*(Bombus Bombus)*
**NEW ZEALAND**

Glimpsed this beauty from my bathroom while on a weekend jaunt to Wellington. He was gnawing on chicken bones. By the time I'd got downstairs with my gun, he'd gone. In my disappointment, I failed to notice that I was completely naked, until a passer-by pointed out my embarrassment.

Tookey's Possum is renowned for its smell, which is described by locals as "a mixture of lavender, honeysuckle, and an open sewer."

### Short-crested Otto
*(Bombus Bombus)*
**FINLAND**

Finland has many lakes, but it is only on the banks of Lake Saimaa that one finds the Short-crested Otto. It was during an off-the-books hunt for the Ringed Seal at Imatra that I spotted the Otto, his magenta plumage clearly visible on the shore. Armed only with four or five of my favourite clubs, I was unable to pick off the bird.

Once riled, it pursued me without mercy until I was forced to undertake the "wasp defence", submerging myself in the lake waters. At this point I was set upon by several ringed seals, and only the intervention of a gentleman in a coracle prevented my demise at their hands. Short crest, short temper, as I told the boys back at the lodge.

### Cubic Salamander
*(Bombus Bombus)*
**PORTUGAL**

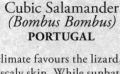

Portugal's hot climate favours the lizard, with his cold blood and scaly skin. While sunbathing upon a rock, not unlike a lizard, I caught sight of this square specimen darting behind a boulder. I reached for my dart gun and pursued him down the beach for a mile, all the while keeping pace and lining up my shot. Just as he paused, I was apprehended by the authorities, as I had strayed from the nude beach to the conventional, clothed bathing area. As I was bundled into the police car, wrapped in a dirty blanket, I could see the Cubic Salamander laughing from a promontory. With luck on my side, I hope one day to craft a pair of bathing trunks from this species.

### Scotch Kitty
*(Bombus Bombus)*
**SCOTLAND (HIGHLANDS)**

Long-fabled but seldom seen, drawings of the Scotch Kitty were dismissed as mere doodles by respected naturalists including Herman Weißgarten and Hennig Plum. And in many ways it does resemble the kind of cat one might draw while on the telephone waiting for an appointment to have cable Internet installed. However, I spied one on Ben Nevis, but did not have a weapon to hand. The beef sandwich I threw at it glanced off its glossy coat with little effect.

### Beaver Wasp
*(Bombus Bombus)*
**PERU**

The mysteries of darkest Peru have confounded many a hunter. From icy mountain to torrid rainforest, it boasts a biodiversity that sends even the most jaded hunter to the gun cupboard with a spring in his step. I will not, however, return to Peru. My encounter with the Beaver Wasp in the province of Madre de Dios, took place not in the boundless kingdom of nature, but rather in my own bedroom. I awoke with a powerful thirst in the night and reached for a glass of water in the dark. But instead of a tumbler of Adam's ale, I grasped a two-foot long insect with duck legs. I managed to avoid its vicious sting only by hiding under the covers, where I remained until my discovery by the hotel maid the next day.

### Herbert
*(Herbertus)*
**FRANCE**

At the end of a long hunting season, with many trophies gained, I retired to the south of France for a little light relaxation. I anticipated a few weeks of wine, boules, bread, and beef.

It was after an evening of all four that I encountered a creature the Provence folk call "Herbert". The less said about this repulsive animal the better, suffice it to say that my meeting with this savage and unpredictable beast left me semi-nude, terrified, and eager to learn more. I cannot say exactly what Herbert is, but I have a healthy respect for it.

# OTHER BOOKS FROM ONI PRESS!

BAD MACHINERY, VOLUME 1:
THE CASE OF THE TEAM SPIRIT
By John Allison
136 pages, softcover, full color
ISBN 978-1-62010-084-4

DIESEL SWEETIES:
I'M A ROCKER. I ROCK OUT.
By R. Stevens
136 pages, softcover, full color
ISBN 978-1-62010-090-5

DOUBLE FINE ACTION COMICS,
VOLUME 1
By Scott C.
128 pages, softcover, b/w & full color
ISBN 978-1-62010-085-1

DOUBLE FINE ACTION COMICS,
VOLUME 2
By Scott C.
120 pages, softcover, b/w & full color
ISBN 978-1-62010-086-8

HOPELESS SAVAGES:
GREATEST HITS 2000-2010
By Jen Van Meter, Christine Norrie,
Bryan Lee O'Malley, Andi Watson,
Chynna Clugston Flores,
Ross Campbell, & More
392 pages, softcover, black and white
ISBN 978-1-934964-48-4

CROGAN'S VENGEANCE
By Chris Schweizer
192 pages, hardcover, black and white
ISBN 978-1-934964-06-4

MERMIN, BOOK 1:
OUT OF WATER
By Joey Weiser
152 pages, hardcover, full color
ISBN 978-1-934964-98-9

SCOTT PILGRIM, VOLUME 1:
PRECIOUS LITTLE LIFE
By Bryan Lee O'Malley
192 pages, hardcover, full color
ISBN 978-1-62010-000-4

COURTNEY CRUMRIN, VOLUME 1:
THE NIGHT THINGS
By Ted Naifeh
136 pages, hardcover, full color
ISBN 978-1-934964-77-4

## BAD MACHINERY

### THE CASE OF THE SIMPLE SOUL

Coming Soon!

ONI PRESS
REVOLUTIONIZE COMICS
www.onipress.com